GROWING TIKTOK FOLLOWERS

CONTENTS

Introduction..................................3

Optimize Your Profile for Maximum Appeal and Discoverabili ty...................5

Create Captivating and Shareable Content.....................................11

Engage with the TikTok Community and Collaborate.................................17

Optimize Your Posting Strategy for Maximum Reach.......................24

Promote Your TikTok Content Beyond the Platform....................31

Conclusion.................................38

INTRODUCTION

In today's digital age, TikTok has emerged as a powerful platform for sharing creative and entertaining content. With its vast user base and incredible potential for virality, many individuals are eager to grow their TikTok followers and expand their reach. In this guide, we will explore effective strategies to increase your TikTok followers. From optimizing your profile and creating captivating content to engaging with the TikTok community and leveraging trending hashtags, we will provide you with valuable tips and techniques to boost your follower count. Whether you're a budding content creator or simply looking to gain more visibility, this guide will equip you with the knowledge to thrive on TikTok.

Step 1
Optimize Your Profile for Maximum Appeal and Discoverability

Your TikTok profile serves as your online identity and the first impression for potential followers. By optimizing your profile, you can enhance its appeal and increase your chances of attracting new followers. Here are some essential steps to get started:

Choose an Engaging Profile Picture: Select a clear and visually appealing profile picture that represents your personal brand or content niche. Make sure it stands out and grabs attention.

Craft a Compelling Bio: Use your bio to introduce yourself, highlight your unique qualities, and express your content theme. Keep it concise, creative, and intriguing, enticing viewers to learn more about you.

Utilize Relevant Keywords: Incorporate relevant keywords related to your niche or the type of content you create. This helps increase the discoverability of your profile when users search for specific topics.

Include Links: TikTok allows you to add clickable links in your profile. Utilize this feature to direct viewers to your other social media accounts, website, or any external platforms related to your content.

Consistency is Key: Maintain a consistent visual style and tone throughout your profile, including your profile picture, bio, and content. This helps create a cohesive and recognizable brand image.

Stay Active and Engaged: Regularly post content and engage with your audience through comments, likes, and shares. This demonstrates your dedication and encourages users to follow you for more exciting updates.

By implementing these profile optimization strategies, you can make your TikTok profile more appealing, increase your discoverability, and lay the foundation for growing your followers. Remember, the key is to create a profile that sparks interest and entices users to hit that "Follow" button.

Step 2
Create Captivating and Shareable Content

Creating captivating and shareable content is vital for growing your TikTok followers. When your videos capture attention and resonate with viewers, they are more likely to engage with your content and become loyal followers. Here are some essential tips to create compelling TikTok content:

Identify Your Target Audience: Understand the preferences, interests, and demographics of your target audience. This knowledge will help you tailor your content to their tastes and increase the chances of gaining followers within your niche.

Embrace Trends and Challenges: Stay updated with the latest TikTok trends and challenges. Participate in popular challenges by putting your unique spin on them. This helps you tap into existing trends and reach a wider audience.

Tell a Story in Seconds: TikTok videos have a short duration, so it's essential to capture attention quickly. Tell a story or convey your message effectively within the first few seconds to engage viewers and make them want to watch the entire video.

Be Authentic and Show Personality: Let your true self shine through in your content. People are drawn to authenticity, so don't be afraid to show your personality, sense of humor, or unique perspective. This helps build a genuine connection with your audience.

Utilize Visual and Audio Effects: TikTok offers a wide range of creative effects, filters, and editing tools. Experiment with these features to enhance the visual appeal of your videos and make them stand out in the crowded TikTok feed.

Use Captions and Text Overlays: Incorporate clear and concise captions or text overlays to complement your video content. This makes it easier for viewers to understand your message, even without sound, and increases shareability.

Remember, the key to creating captivating content is to experiment, analyze audience responses, and adapt accordingly. Stay creative, stay true to your style, and continuously innovate to keep your TikTok followers engaged and entertained.

Step 3
Engage with the TikTok Community and Collaborate

Engaging with the TikTok community is crucial for growing your followers and building a strong presence on the platform. By actively participating in the community, you can increase your visibility, gain followers, and establish valuable connections. Here are essential steps to boost your engagement and collaboration:

Respond to Comments and Messages: Take the time to reply to comments and messages from your followers. Engaging with your audience shows that you value their support and creates a sense of community around your content.

Follow and Interact with Relevant Accounts: Identify influencers, creators, and accounts in your niche or with similar content. Follow them and engage with their posts through likes, comments, and shares. This can help attract their followers' attention and potentially lead to collaborations.

Collaborate with Other TikTokers: Collaborations are an excellent way to cross-promote and tap into each other's audiences. Seek out creators who align with your content style or have complementary interests. Collaborative videos or duets can expand your reach and attract new followers.

Participate in TikTok Challenges and Hashtag Trends: Joining popular challenges and using relevant hashtags can increase the visibility of your content. It allows you to reach a wider audience and potentially gain followers who are actively participating in those trends.

Engage in TikTok Live: Utilize TikTok Live to interact with your followers in real-time. Host Q&A sessions, share behind-the-scenes glimpses, or provide live tutorials. This direct engagement helps foster a deeper connection with your audience.

Share TikTok on Other Platforms: Cross-promote your TikTok content on other social media platforms like Instagram, Twitter, or YouTube. Direct your existing followers to your TikTok profile, encouraging them to follow you on TikTok as well.

By actively engaging with the TikTok community, collaborating with other creators, and participating in challenges, you can significantly increase your exposure and attract more followers. Remember to be genuine, supportive, and consistent in your interactions, fostering a positive and engaging environment for your audience.

Step 4
Optimize Your Posting Strategy for Maximum Reach

To grow your TikTok followers effectively, it's important to optimize your posting strategy. By understanding the best times to post, leveraging TikTok's algorithm, and utilizing analytics, you can maximize your reach and increase the likelihood of attracting new followers. Here are some key steps to optimize your posting strategy:

Analyze Your TikTok Analytics: Take advantage of TikTok's built-in analytics tools to gain insights into your audience demographics, video performance, and follower growth. Analyze this data to identify trends, understand what content resonates with your audience, and tailor your future posts accordingly.

Post Consistently: Establish a consistent posting schedule that works for you and your audience. Regularly uploading new content keeps your followers engaged and increases your chances of appearing in the For You page, where you can attract new followers.

Experiment with Post Timing: Test different posting times to identify when your content receives the most engagement. Consider factors like your target audience's timezone and their likely browsing habits. Use TikTok's analytics to track the performance of your posts at various times and adjust your strategy accordingly.

Quality over Quantity: While consistency is important, prioritize quality content over sheer volume. Aim to create high-quality videos that captivate and resonate with your audience. Compelling and well-produced content is more likely to be shared, leading to increased visibility and follower growth.

Utilize TikTok's Features: Take advantage of TikTok's features like sounds, effects, and filters to enhance the appeal of your videos. Experiment with trending effects or create your own unique style to stand out from the crowd.

Engage with Trending Topics: Stay up-to-date with current events, holidays, and popular trends. Create content that relates to these topics and incorporates relevant hashtags. By participating in trending conversations, you can tap into the broader TikTok community and attract new followers.

By optimizing your posting strategy, you can increase your visibility, improve engagement, and ultimately grow your TikTok followers. Stay informed about your audience, create high-quality content consistently, and leverage TikTok's features and trends to maximize your reach and impact.

Step 5
Promote Your TikTok Content Beyond the Platform

To accelerate the growth of your TikTok followers, it's essential to promote your TikTok content beyond the platform itself. By leveraging other online channels and collaborating with influencers, you can expand your reach, attract new followers, and build a strong online presence. Here are some effective strategies for promoting your TikTok content:

Share TikTok Videos on Other Social Media Platforms: Cross-promote your TikTok content on platforms like Instagram, Twitter, Facebook, or YouTube. Share snippets, previews, or links to your TikTok videos, enticing your existing followers to join you on TikTok.

Embed TikTok Videos on Your Website or Blog: If you have a personal website, blog, or any online presence, embed your TikTok videos to showcase your content to a broader audience. This can attract visitors who may not be active on TikTok and encourage them to follow you.

Collaborate with Influencers: Partner with influencers in your niche or with a similar target audience. Collaborative videos, shoutouts, or mentions from popular TikTokers can expose your content to a larger follower base and increase your chances of gaining new followers.

Engage with Other Social Media Communities: Participate in relevant online communities, such as Facebook groups, Reddit threads, or forums, where your target audience is active. Share your TikTok content in a non-spammy manner and engage in conversations related to your niche. This can pique the interest of potential followers and drive them to your TikTok profile.

Utilize Your Email List: If you have an email list, include links or previews of your TikTok videos in your newsletters or promotional emails. This can notify your existing subscribers about your TikTok presence and encourage them to follow you.

Collaborate with Brands or Businesses: Seek collaborations with brands or businesses that align with your content or target audience. This can involve creating sponsored content, featuring their products/services in your videos, or participating in branded challenges. Such collaborations can expose your content to a wider audience and potentially gain new followers.

By promoting your TikTok content beyond the platform, you can tap into different online communities, engage with influencers, and reach potential followers who may not be active TikTok users. Remember to strategically select your promotion channels, maintain consistency in your messaging, and provide compelling reasons for viewers to follow you on TikTok.

CONCLUSION

Growing your TikTok followers requires a combination of strategic tactics and consistent effort. By optimizing your profile, creating captivating content, engaging with the TikTok community, optimizing your posting strategy, and promoting your content beyond the platform, you can significantly increase your follower count. Remember to stay authentic, understand your target audience, and adapt to trends and challenges. Consistency and quality should be prioritized over quantity, and leveraging TikTok's features and analytics will help you refine your content strategy. Additionally, collaborations with influencers and cross-promotion on other social media platforms can expand your reach and attract new followers. With dedication, creativity, and a strong understanding of your audience, you can successfully grow your TikTok followers and build a thriving presence on this dynamic platform.

www.ingramcontent.com/pod-product-compliance
Lightning Source LLC
Chambersburg PA
CBHW070141230526
45472CB00004B/1632